Love, all alike, no season knows, nor clime,
Nor hours, age, months, which are the rags of time.

John Donne

First published 1997
This edition © Robert Frederick Ltd. 1997
4, North Parade Buildings, Bath BA1 1LF, England

Editorial selections © Robert Frederick Ltd. All rights reserved.

Printed by Man Sang Envelope Manufacturing Co. Ltd., China

The Wedding Book

*the story of our marriage
with illustrations and verse and prose in celebration of love*

The Engagement

Use the pages throughout this book to record your own special memories

" All love is sweet,
Given or returned. Common as light is love,
And its familiar voice wearies not ever."

Shelley

The Engagement

tread softly

I have spread my dreams under your feet:
Tread softly, because you tread on my dreams.

William Butler Yeats

Pre-Wedding Celebrations

Hen Parties, Stag Nights or anything else your imagination ran to . . .

Sonnet XLIII,
From The Portuguese

How do I love thee? Let me count the ways.
I love thee to the depth and breadth and height
My soul can reach, when feeling out of sight,
For the ends of Being and ideal Grace.
I love thee to the level of every day's
Most quiet need, by sun and candlelight.
I love thee freely, as men strive for Right;
I love thee purely, as they turn from Praise.
I love thee with the passion put to use
In my old griefs, and with my childhood's faith.
I love thee with a love I seemed to lose
With my lost saints, – I love thee with the breath,
Smiles, tears, of all my life! – and, if God choose,
I shall but love thee better after death.

Elizabeth Barrett Browning

The Bridal Party

Include details of outfits, flowers, accessories etc

*"A happy bridesmaid makes
a happy bride."*
Lord Tennyson

The Bridal Party

The Bridal Party

Who, being loved, is poor?

Oscar Wilde

The Wedding Guests

"All other things to their destruction draw,
Only our love hath no decay;
This, no tomorrow hath, nor yesterday,
Running it never runs from us away,
But truly keeps his first, last, everlasting day."

John Donne

first, last, everlasting day

The Wedding Guests

The Wedding Guests

Sometimes when one person is missing, the whole world seems depopulated.

Lamartine

The Ceremony

Include details of venue, order of service, music, transport, flowers etc

"Love is, above all, the gift of oneself."

Jean Anouilh

One word
Frees us of all the weight
and pain of life:
That word is love.

Sophocles

The Ceremony

"The love we give away is the only love we keep."

Elbert Hubbard

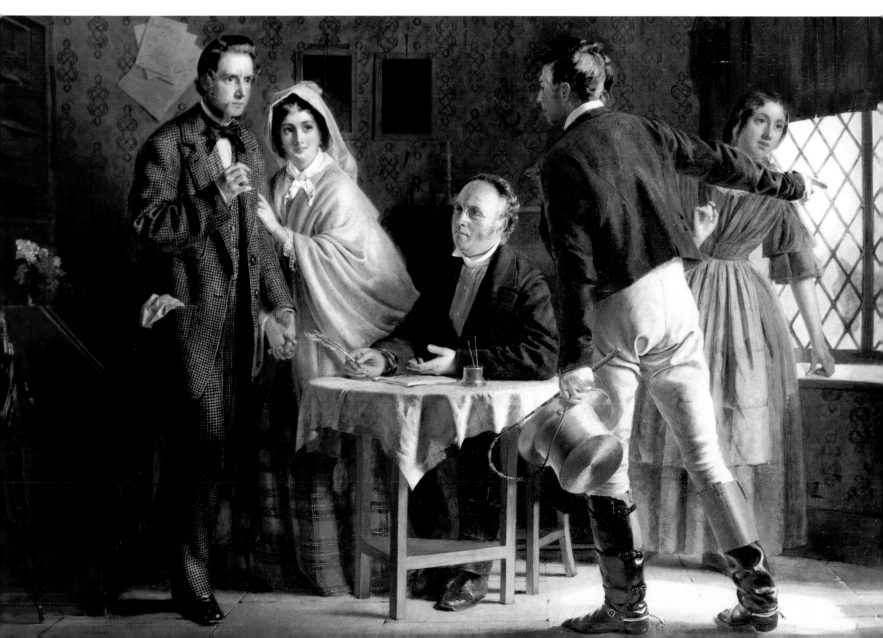

The Ceremony

"For an instant, love can transform the world."

Author Unidentified

The Reception

Include details of venue, menu, speeches, telegrams, entertainment, gifts, special touches, etc

The Reception

"An ideal wife is any woman who has an ideal husband."

Booth Tarkington

The Reception

We are all born for love; it is the principle of existence and its only end.

Benjamin Disraeli

The Reception

a promise more precise

A kiss, when all is said, what is it?
An oath that's given closer than before;
A promise more precise; the sealing of
Confessions that till then were barely breathed;
A rosy dot placed on the *i* in loving;
A secret that is confined to a mouth and not to ears.

from Cyrano de Bergerac by Edmond Rostand

Wedding Gifts

Gift ....

From ....

Gift ....

From ....

Gift ....

From ....

Gift ....

From ....

Gift ....

From ....

Gift ....

From ....

Gift ....

From ....

Gift ....

From ....

Gift ....

From ....

Gift ....

From ....

Gift ....

From ....

Gift ....

From ....

Gift ....

From ....

. . . for my sake, sweet, let the few years go by; we are married, and my arms are round you, and my face touches yours, and I am asking you, Were you not to me, in that dim beginning of 1846, a joy behind all joys, a life added to and transforming mine, the good I choose from all the possible gifts of God on this earth, for which I seemed to have lived . . . '

Robert Browning to Elizabeth Barrett

a joy behind all joys

Wedding Gifts

Gift ....

From ....

Gift ....

From ....

Gift ....

From ....

Gift ....

From ....

Gift ....

From ....

Gift ....

From ....

Gift ....

From ....

Gift ....

From ....

Wedding Gifts

Gift ....

From ....

Gift ....

From ....

Gift ....

From ....

Gift ....

From ....

Gift ....

From ....

Gift ....

From ....

Gift ....

From ....

Gift ....

From ....

Gift ....

From ....

Gift ....

From ....

Gift ....

From ....

Gift ....

From ....

Wedding Gifts

Gift ....
From ....

Gift ....
From ....

Gift ....
From ....

Gift ....
From ....

Gift ....
From ....

Gift ....
From ....

Gift ....
From ....

Gift ....
From ....

Gift ....
From ....

Gift ....
From ....

Gift ....
From ....

Gift ....
From ....

Gift ....
From ....

Wedding Gifts

Gift ....

From ....

Gift ....

From ....

Gift ....

From ....

Gift ....

From ....

Gift ....

From ....

Gift ....

From ....

Gift ....

From ....

Gift ....

From ....

Gift ....

From ....

Gift ....

From ....

Gift ....

From ....

Gift ....

From ....

Gift ....

From ....

"Gratitude is the heart's memory."
French Proverb

Wedding Gifts

Gift ....

From ....

Gift ....

From ....

Gift ....

From ....

Gift ....

From ....

Gift ....

From ....

Gift ....

From ....

Gift ....

From ....

Gift ....

From ....

Gift ....

From ....

Gift ....

From ....

Gift ....

From ....

Wedding Gifts

Gift ....

From ....

Gift ....

From ....

"Love is an act of endless forgiveness, a tender look which becomes a habit."

Peter Ustinov

Gift ....

From ....

Gift ....

From ....

Wedding Gifts

Gift ....

From ....

Gift ....

From ....

Gift ....

From ....

Gift ....

From ....

Gift ....

From ....

Gift ....

From ....

Gift ....

From ....

Gift ....

From ....

Gift ....

From ....

Gift ....

From ....

Gift ....

From ....

Gift ....

From ....

Gift ....

From ....

The Honeymoon

Record those special memories surrounding your first weeks together

"Love does not consist in gazing at each other,
but in looking together in the same direction."

Saint-Exupéry

We two form a multitude.

Author Unidentified

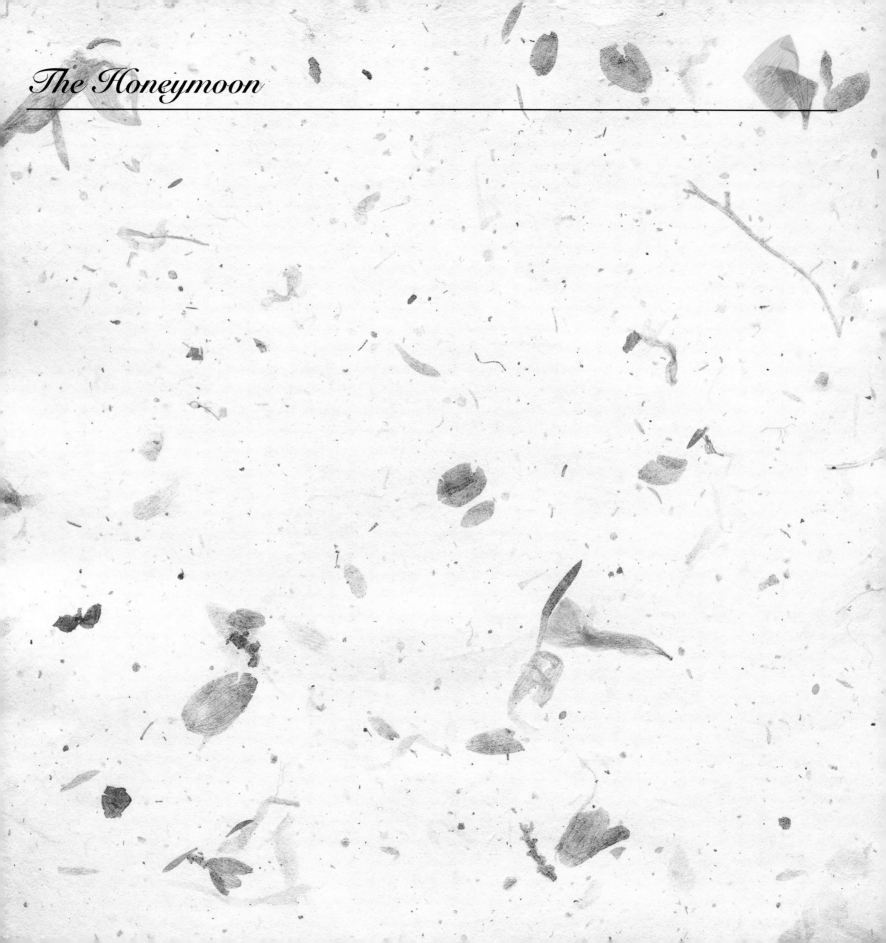

The Honeymoon

The Honeymoon

greet as angels greet

Though seas and land
betwixt us both
Our faith and troth,
Like separated souls,
All time and space controls:
Above the highest sphere we meet,
Unseen, unknown;
and greet as angels greet.

Richard Lovelace

Special Memories

Use these pages to keep a record of other personal and special memories surrounding your wedding and the start of your new life together

"Bliss in possession will not last;
Remembered joys are never past."

James Montgomery

Sonnet

I wish I could remember that first day,
First hour, first moment of your meeting me,
If bright or dim the season, it might be
Summer or Winter for aught I can say;
So unrecorded did it slip away,
So blind was I to see and to foresee,
So dull to mark the budding of my tree
That would not blossom yet for many a May.
If only I could recollect it, such
A day o days! I let it come and go
As traceless as a thaw of bygone snow;
It seemed to mean so little, meant so much;
If only now I could recall that touch,
First touch of hand in hand –
Did one but know!

Christina Rossetti

first hour, first moment

Special Memories

"The ring, so worn as you behold,
So thin, so pale, is yet of gold.
The passion such it was to prove
Worn with life's care, love yet was love."

George Crabbe

Special Memories

Unable are the Loved to die
For Love is Immortality.

Emily Dickinson

Acknowledgements

Pg 5,23 Signing of the Register by Edmund Blair Leighton (1853-1922), City of Bristol Museum and Art Gallery/Brigeman Art Library, London; Pg 6 The Proposal by Alfred W Elmore, Christie's Photo Library, London; Pg 8 The Empress Comes (or "Poppea Comes") by George Lawrence (1858-1933), Sotheby's Picture Library; Pg 10,11 The Prince's Choice by Thomas Reynolds Lamont (1826-1898), Sotheby's Picture Library; Pg 12 The Bridesmaid by Philip Richard Morris (1838-1902), Christopher Wood Gallery, London/Bridgeman Art Library, London; Pg 15 The Wedding Dress by George Goodwin Kilburne (1839-1924), Phillips, The International Fine Art Auctioneers/Bridgeman Art Library, London; Pg 16,17 Fresh from the Altar by Jessica Hayllar (1858-1940), Christie's, London/Bridgeman Art Library, London; Pg 18 Rosaline (Woman with Roses) by Hugh de Twenebroke Glazebrook (1855-1937), Christies Photo Library, London; Pg 21 Paolo and Francesca by Dante Gabriel Rossetti (1828-82); Pg 24,25 Wedding Bells by James Hayllar (1829-1920), John Noott Galleries, Broadway, Worcs./Bridgeman Art Library, London; Pg 26 A Wedding at Gretna Green by Jerry Barrett (1824-1906), Christopher Wood Gallery, London/Bridgeman Art Library, London; Pg 28,29 The Wedding Meal at Yport by Albert-Auguste Fourie (b.1854), Musée des Beaux-Arts, Rouen/Bridgeman Art Library, London; Pg 31 The Wedding Breakfast by Frederick Daniel Hardy (1826-1911), Atkinson Art Gallery, Southport, Lancs/Bridgeman Art Library, London; Pg 32,33 Changing Homes by George Elgar Hicks (1824-1914), Geffrye Museum, London/Bridgeman Art Library, London; Pg 34,35 La Belle Dame Sans Merci by Sir Frank Dicksee (1853-1928), City of Bristol Museum and Art Library/Bridgeman Art Library, London; Pg 36 Her Wedding Day by Anton Weiss (1801-51), Christie's, London/Bridgeman Art Library, London; Pg 38 The Poets Theme by John Callcott Horsley (1817-1903), Sotheby's Picture Library; Pg 39 Till Death Do Us Part by Edmund Blair Leighton (1853-1922), Forbes Magazine Collection, New York/Bridgeman Art Library, London; Pg 40,41 A Venetian Wedding by Roda G Puig, IFI (1900), Christie's, London/Bridgeman Art Library, London; Pg 43 The Year's at Spring, All's right with the World by Sir Lawrence Alma-Tadema (1836-1912), Sotheby's Picture Library; Pg 44,45 The Coming Event by Jessica Hayllar (1858-1940), Forbes Magazine Collection, New York /Christie's Photo Library, London; Pg 47 Wedding in Aragon by Juan Pablo Salinas (1871-1946), Josef Mensing Gallery, Hamm-Rhynern/Bridgeman Art Library, London; Pg 48,49 The Awakening of Love by Gustave Schmatz Herbert, Christies Photo Library, London; Pg 50,51 Where Next? by Edward Frederick Brewtnall (1846-1902), Sotheby's Picture Library; Pg 52 Hesperus by Sir Joseph Noel Paton (1821-1901), Glasgow Art Gallery and Museum/Bridgeman Art Library, London; Pg 55 The Shrine by John William Waterhouse (1849-1917), Christopher Wood Gallery, London/Bridgeman Art Library, London; Pg 56 Call to Arms by Edmund Blair Leighton (1853-1922), Roy Miles Gallery, 29 Bruton Street, London W1/Bridgeman Art Library, London; Pg 58 Le Moulin de la Galette by Auguste Renoir; Pg 59 The Measure for the Wedding Ring, 1855, by Michael Frederick Halliday (1822-1869), Private Collection/Bridgeman Art Library, London; Pg 60 The Love Letter by John William Godward (1861-1922), The Maas Gallery, London/Bridgeman Art Library, London

Other images © Robert Frederick Ltd. 1996